HOW TO BECOME A HAPPY PERSON :
Guide for living a happier life

JAVIER S.GREGORY

TABLE OF CONTENT

Chapter 1

What Is Happiness?
Happiness is something that people seek to find, yet what defines happiness can vary from one person to the next. When most people talk about the true meaning of happiness, they might be talking about how they feel in the present moment or referring to a more general sense of how they feel about life overall.

Happiness Definition:
Happiness is an emotional state characterized by feelings of joy, satisfaction, contentment, and fulfillment. While happiness has many different definitions, it is often described as involving positive emotions and life satisfaction.

Because happiness tends to be such a broadly defined term, psychologists and other social scientists typically use the term 'subjective well-being' when they talk about this emotional state. Just as it sounds, subjective well-being tends to focus on an individual's overall personal feelings about their life in the present.

Two key components of happiness (or subjective well-being) are:

- The balance of emotions: Everyone experiences both positive and negative emotions, feelings, and moods. Happiness is generally linked to experiencing more positive feelings than negative ones.
- Life satisfaction: This relates to how satisfied you feel with different areas of your life including your relationships, work, achievements, and other things that you consider important.

Another definition of happiness comes from the ancient philosopher Aristotle, who suggested that happiness is the one human desire, and all other human desires exist as a way to obtain happiness. He believed that there were four levels of happiness: happiness from immediate gratification, comparison, and achievement, from making positive contributions, and from achieving fulfillment.

Happiness, Aristotle suggested, could be achieved through the golden mean, which involves finding a balance between deficiency and excess.1

Signs of Happiness
While perceptions of happiness may be different from one person to the next, there are some key signs that psychologists look for when measuring and assessing happiness.

Some key signs of happiness include:

1. Feeling like you are living the life you wanted
2. Going with the flow and a willingness to take life as it comes

3. Feeling that the conditions of your life are good
4. Enjoying positive, healthy relationships with other people
5. Feeling that you have accomplished (or will accomplish) what you want in life
6. Feeling satisfied with your life
7. Feeling positive more than negative
8. Being open to new ideas and experiences
9. Practicing self-care and treating yourself with kindness and compassion
10. Experiencing gratitude
11. Feeling that you are living life with a sense of meaning and purpose
12. Wanting to share your happiness and joy with others

One important thing to remember is that happiness isn't a state of constant euphoria. Instead, happiness is an overall sense of experiencing more positive emotions than negative ones.

Happy people still feel the whole range of human emotions—anger, frustration, boredom, loneliness, and even sadness—from time to time. But even when faced with discomfort, they have an underlying sense of optimism that things will get better, that they can deal with what is happening, and that they will be able to feel happy again.

Types of Happiness
There are many different ways of thinking about happiness. For example, the ancient Greek philosopher Aristotle made a distinction between two different kinds of happiness: hedonic and eudaimonia.

1. Hedonia: Hedonic happiness is derived from pleasure. It is most often associated with doing what feels good, self-care, fulfilling desires, experiencing enjoyment, and feeling a sense of satisfaction.
2. Eudaimonia: This type of happiness is derived from seeking virtue and meaning.

Important components of eudaimonic well-being include feeling that your life has meaning, value, and purpose. It is associated more with fulfilling responsibilities, investing in long-term goals, being a concern for the welfare of other people, and living up to personal ideals.

Hedonia and eudemonia are more commonly known today in psychology as pleasure and meaning, respectively. More recently, psychologists have suggested the addition of the third component that relates to engagement. These are feelings of commitment and participation in different areas of life.

Research suggests that happy people tend to rank pretty high on eudaimonic life satisfaction and better than average on their hedonic life satisfaction.2

All of these can play an important role in the overall experience of happiness, although the relative value of each can be highly subjective. Some activities may be both pleasurable and meaningful, while others might skew more one way or the other.

For example, volunteering for a cause you believe in might be more meaningful than pleasurable. Watching your favorite tv show, on the other hand, might rank lower in meaning and higher on pleasure.3

Some types of happiness that may fall under these three main categories include:

3. Joy: A often relatively brief feeling that is felt in the present moment
Excitement: A happy feeling that involves looking forward to something with positive anticipation
Gratitude: A positive emotion that involves being thankful and appreciative
Pride: A feeling of satisfaction in something that you have accomplished

4. Optimism: This is a way of looking at life with a positive, upbeat outlook

5. Contentment: This type of happiness involves a sense of satisfaction

How to Cultivate Happiness

While some people just tend to be naturally happier, there are things that you can do to cultivate your sense of happiness.

1. Pursue Intrinsic Goals

Achieving goals that you are intrinsically motivated to pursue, particularly ones that are focused on personal growth and community, can help boost happiness. Research suggests that pursuing these types of intrinsically-motivated goals can increase happiness more than pursuing extrinsic goals like gaining money or status.4

2. Enjoy the Moment

Studies have found that people tend to over earn—they become so focused on accumulating things that they lose track of actually enjoying what they are doing

So, rather than falling into the trap of mindlessly accumulating to the detriment of your happiness, focus on practicing gratitude for the things you have and enjoying the process as you go.

3. Reframe Negative Thoughts

When you find yourself stuck in a pessimistic outlook or experiencing negativity, look for ways that you can reframe your thoughts more positively.

People have a natural negativity bias, or a tendency to pay more attention to bad things than to good things. This can have an impact on everything from how you make decisions to how you form impressions of other people. Discounting the positive—a cognitive distortion where people focus on the negative and ignore the positive—can also contribute to negative thoughts.

Reframing these negative perceptions isn't about ignoring the bad. Instead, it means trying to take a more balanced, realistic look at events. It allows you to notice patterns in your thinking and then challenge negative thoughts.

Impact of Happiness
Why is happiness so important?

Happiness has been shown to predict positive outcomes in many different areas of life including mental well-being, physical health, and overall longevity.

1. Positive emotions increase satisfaction with life.
2. Happiness helps people build stronger coping skills and emotional resources.
3. Positive emotions are linked to better health and longevity. One study found that people who experienced more positive emotions than negative ones were more likely to have survived over 13 years.

4. Positive feelings increase resilience. Resilience helps people better manage stress and bounce back better when faced with setbacks. For example, one study found that happier people tend to have lower levels of the stress hormone cortisol and that these benefits tend to persist over time.

People who report having a positive state of well-being are more likely to engage in healthy behaviors such as eating fruits and vegetables and engaging in regular physical exercise.8

Being happy may make help you get sick less often. Happier mental states are linked to increased immunity.

How to Be a Happier Person

Some people seem to have a naturally higher baseline for happiness—one large-scale study of more than 2,000 twins suggested that around 50% of overall life satisfaction was due to genetics, 10% to external events, and 40% to individual activities.

So while you might not be able to control what your "base level" of happiness is, there are things that you can do to make your life happier and more fulfilling. Even the happiest of individuals can feel down from time to time and happiness is something that all people need to consciously pursue.

Cultivate Strong Relationships
Social support is an essential part of well-being. Research has found that good social relationships are the strongest predictor of happiness. Having positive and supportive connections with people you care about can provide a buffer against stress, improve your health, and help you become a happier person.

In the Harvard Study of Adult Development, a longitudinal study that looked at participants over 80 years, researchers found that relationships and how happy people are in those relationships strongly impacted overall health.11

So if you are trying to improve your happiness, cultivating solid social connections is a great place to start. Consider deepening your existing relationships and exploring ways to make new friends.

Get Regular Exercise
Exercise is good for both your body and mind. Physical activity is linked to a range of physical and psychological benefits including improved mood. Numerous studies have shown that regular exercise may play a role in warding off symptoms of depression, but evidence also suggests that it may also help make people happier, too.

In one analysis of past research on the connection between physical activity and happiness, researchers found a consistent positive link.

Even a little bit of exercise produces a happiness boost—people who were physically active for as little as 10 minutes a day or who worked out only once a week had higher levels of happiness than people who never exercised.

Show Gratitude
In one study, participants were asked to engage in a writing exercise for 10 to 20 minutes each night before bed. Some were instructed to write about daily hassles, some about neutral events, and some about things they were grateful for. The results found that people who had written about gratitude had increased positive emotions, increased subjective happiness, and improved life satisfaction.

As the authors of the study suggest, keeping a gratitude list is a relatively easy, affordable, simple, and pleasant way to boost your mood. Try setting aside a few minutes each night to write down or think about things in your life that you are grateful for.

Why You Should Write Down the Things You're Grateful for Each Day

Find a Sense of Purpose

Research has found that people who feel like they have a purpose have better well-being and feel more fulfilled. A sense of purpose involves seeing your life as having goals, direction, and meaning. It may help improve happiness by promoting healthier behaviors.

Some things you can do to help find a sense of purpose include:

Explore your interests and passions
Engage in prosocial and altruistic causes
Work to address injustices
Look for new things you might want to learn more about
This sense of purpose is influenced by a variety of factors, but it is also something that you can cultivate. It involves finding a goal that you care deeply about that will lead

you to engage in productive, positive actions
to work toward that goal.

Chapter 2

Daily habits
The following daily habits may help you achieve more happiness in your life.

1. Smile
You tend to smile when you're happy. But it's a two-way street.

We smile because we're happy, and smiling causes the brain to release dopamine, which makes us happier.

While not completely foolproof, researchers have found that the link between smiling and happiness could be attributed to the "facial feedback hypothesis," where facial expressions may have a modest influence on emotions.

That does not mean you have to go around with a fake smile plastered on your face all the time. But the next time you find yourself feeling low, crack a smile and see what happens. Or try starting each morning by smiling at yourself in the mirror.

2. Exercise

Exercise isn't just for your body. Regular exercise can help reduce stress, feelings of anxiety, and symptoms of depression while boosting self-esteem and happiness.

Even a small amount of physical activity can make a difference. You don't have to train for a triathlon or scale a cliff — unless that's what makes you happy, of course.

The trick is to not overexert yourself. If you suddenly throw yourself into a strenuous routine, you may just end up frustrated (and sore).

Consider these exercise starters:

Take a walk around the block every night after dinner.
Start your day with 5 minutes of stretching.
Remind yourself of any fun activities you once enjoyed but that have fallen by the wayside. Or you could consider starting activities you always wanted to try, such as golf, bowling, or dancing.

3. Get plenty of sleep
Most adults need at least 7 hours of trusted Source of sleep every night. If you find yourself fighting the urge to nap during the day or just generally feel like you're in a fog, your body may be telling you it needs more rest.

No matter how much our modern society steers us toward less sleep, we know that adequate sleep is a vital trusted Source of good health, brain function, and emotional well-being. Getting enough sleep also reduces your riskTrusted Source of developing certain chronic illnesses, such as heart disease, depression, and diabetes.

Here are a few tips to help you build a better sleep routine:

Write down how many hours of sleep you get each night and how rested you feel. After a week, you should have a better idea of how you're doing. You can also try using an app to track your sleep.
Go to bed and wake up at the same time every day, including on weekends.
Reserve the hour before bed as quiet time. Take a bath, read, or do something relaxing. Avoid heavy eating and drinking.
Keep your bedroom dark, cool, and quiet.
Invest in some good bedding.
If you have to take a nap, try limiting it to 20 minutes.
If you consistently have problems sleeping, consider talking with a doctor. You may

have a sleep disorder that requires treatment.

4. Eat with the mood in mind
You may already know that your food choices have an impact on your overall physical health. But some foods can also affect your state of mind. Trusted Source

For example:

Carbohydrates release serotonin, a "feel good" hormone. Just keep simple carbs — foods high in sugar and starch — to a minimum because that energy surge is short and you'll crash. Choosing complex carbs, such as vegetables, beans, and whole grains, can help you avoid a crash while still providing serotonin.
Lean meat, poultry, legumes, and dairy are high in protein. Protein-rich foods release dopamine and norepinephrine, which boost energy and concentration.

Omega-3 fatty acids, such as those found in fatty fish, have been found to have anti-inflammatory effects trusted Source that extends to your overall brain health. If you don't eat fish, you might consider talking with a doctor about possible supplementation.

Highly processed or deep-fried foods tend to leave you feeling down and so will skipping meals.

If you want to eat with your mood in mind, consider starting with making one food choice for your mood each day.

For example, swap a big, sweet breakfast pastry for some Greek yogurt with fruit. You'll still satisfy your sweet tooth, and the protein will help you avoid a mid-morning energy crash. Consider adding in a new food swap each week.

5. Practice gratitude

Simply being grateful can give your mood a big boost, among other benefits. For example, a two-part study found that practicing gratitude can have a significant impact on feelings of hope and happiness.

You might try starting each day by acknowledging one thing you're grateful for. You can do this while you're brushing your teeth or just waiting for that snoozed alarm to go off.

As you go about your day, consider keeping an eye out for pleasant things in your life. They can be big things, such as knowing that someone loves you or getting a well-deserved promotion.

But they can also be little things, such as a co-worker who offered you a cup of coffee or the neighbor who waved to you. Maybe it could even just be the warmth of the sun on your skin.

With a little practice, you may even become more aware of all the positive things around you.

6. Give a compliment
Research shows that performing acts of kindness may also help promote your overall well-being.

Giving a sincere compliment is a quick, easy way to brighten someone's day while giving your happiness a boost.

Catch the person's eye and say it with a smile so they know you mean it. You might be surprised by how good it makes you feel.

If you want to offer someone a compliment on their physical appearance, make sure to do it respectfully.

7. Breathe deeply

You're tense, your shoulders are tight, and you feel as though you just might "lose it." We all know that feeling.

Instinct may tell you to take a long, deep breath to calm yourself down.

Turns out, that instinct is a good one. ResearchTrusted Source supports the fact that slow breathing and deep breathing exercises can help reduce stress.

The next time you feel stressed or are at your wit's end, work through these steps:

Close your eyes. Try to envision a happy memory or beautiful place.
Take a slow, deep breath through your nose.
Slowly breathe out through your mouth or nose.
Repeat this process several times until you start to feel yourself calm down.

If you're having a hard time taking slow, deliberate breaths, try counting to 5 in your head with each inhale and exhale.

8. Acknowledge the unhappy moments
A positive attitude is generally a good thing, but bad things happen to everyone. It's just part of life.

If you get some bad news, make a mistake, or just feel like you're in a funk, don't try to pretend you're happy.

Acknowledge the feeling of unhappiness, letting yourself experience it for a moment. Then shift your focus toward what made you feel this way and what it might take to recover.

Would a deep breathing exercise help? A long walk outside? Talking it over with someone?

Let the moment pass and take care of yourself. Remember, no one's happy all the time.

9. Keep a journal
A journal is a good way to organize your thoughts, analyze your feelings, and make plans. And you don't have to be a literary genius or write volumes to benefit.

It can be as simple as jotting down a few thoughts before you go to bed. If putting certain things in writing makes you nervous, you can always shred it when you've finished. It's the process that counts.

Not sure what to do with all the feelings that end up on the page? Our guide to organizing your feelings may help.

10. Face stress head-on
Life is full of stressors, and it's impossible to avoid all of them.

There's no need to. Stress isn't always harmful, and we can even change our attitudes about stress. Sometimes, there's an upside to stress.

For those stressors you can't avoid, remind yourself that everyone has stress — there's no reason to think it's all on you. And chances are, you're stronger than you might think you are.

Instead of letting yourself get overwhelmed, try to address the stressor head-on. This might mean initiating an uncomfortable conversation or putting in some extra work, but the sooner you confront it, the sooner the pit in your stomach may start to shrink.

11. Avoid comparing yourself to others
Whether it happens on social media, at work, or even at a yoga class, it's easy to fall into a place where you're comparing yourself to others. The result? You may experience trusted Source more discontent,

lower self-esteem, and even depression and anxiety.

It can take practice to stop comparing yourself to others, but it's worth it for the benefit of having your inner peace and happiness.

You can start with some of the other tips on this list that can help draw your attention inward to yourself, such as deep breathing and journaling. You may also consider talking with a therapist for perspective.

Weekly habits
The following tips include weekly habits that may help you feel happier.

12. Declutter
Decluttering sounds like a big project, but setting aside just 20 minutes a week can have a big impact.

What can you do in 20 minutes? Lots.

Set a timer on your phone and take 15 minutes to tidy up a specific area of one room — say, your closet or that out-of-control junk drawer. Put everything in its place and toss or give away any extra clutter that's not serving you anymore.

Keep a designated box for giveaways to make things a little easier (and avoid creating more clutter).

Use the remaining 5 minutes to do a quick walk through your living space, putting away whatever stray items end up in your path.

You can do this trick once a week, once a day, or anytime you feel like your space is getting out of control.

13. See friends
Humans are largely considered social beings, and while the research is a fixed

trusted Source on how exactly socialization impacts happiness, the consensus is that having social relationships can make us happy.

Who do you miss? Reach out to them. Make a date to get together or simply have a long phone chat.

In adulthood, it can feel next to impossible to make new friends. But it's not about how many friends you have. It's about having meaningful relationships — even if it's just with one or two people.

Try getting involved in a local volunteer group or taking a class. Both can help connect you with like-minded people in your area. And it's likely they're looking for friends, too.

Companionship doesn't have to be limited to other humans. Pets can offer similar benefits, according to multiple studies.

Love animals but can't have a pet? Consider volunteering at a local animal shelter to make some new friends — both human and animal.

14. Plan your week
Feel like you're flailing about? Try sitting down at the end of every week and making a basic list for the following week.

Even if you don't stick to the plan, blocking out time when you can do laundry, go grocery shopping, or tackle projects at work can help quiet your mind.

You can get a fancy planner or app, but even a sticky note on your computer or a piece of scrap paper in your pocket can do the job.

15. Ditch your phone
Unplug. Really.

There's mounting evidence to support the fact that excessive phone use can lead to changes in the brain and impact your mood, with one review even revealing more serious cognitive and emotional changes in adolescents and young adults.

Turn off all the electronics and put those earbuds away for at least 1 hour once a week. They'll still be there for you later if you want them.

If you haven't unplugged in a while, you might be surprised at the difference it makes. Let your mind wander free for a change. Read. Meditate. Take a walk and pay attention to your surroundings. Be sociable. Or be alone. Just be.

Sound too daunting? Try unplugging for a shorter amount of time several times a week.

16. Get into nature

Spending 30 minutes or more a week in green spaces can help lower blood pressure and the chances of developing depression, according to one study trusted Source.

Your green space could be anything such as your neighborhood park, your backyard, or a rooftop garden — anywhere you can appreciate and enjoy nature and fresh air.

Better yet, add some outdoor exercise into the mix for extra benefit. The same aforementioned study found that people who spent time in green spaces were also more likely to exercise more frequently and for longer each time.

17. Explore meditation
There are many methods of meditation to explore. They can involve movement, focus, spirituality, or a combination of all three.

Meditation doesn't have to be complicated. It can be as simple as sitting quietly with your thoughts for 5 minutes. Even the deep breathing exercises mentioned earlier can serve as a form of meditation.

18. Consider therapy

We're certainly happier when we learn how to cope with obstacles. When you're faced with a problem, think about what got you through something similar in the past. Would it work here? What else can you try?

If you feel like you're hitting a brick wall, consider speaking with a mental health professional like a therapist every week. You don't need to have a diagnosed mental health condition or overwhelming crisis to seek therapy.

Mental health professionals are trained to help people improve their coping skills. Plus, there's no obligation to continue once you start.

Even just a few sessions can help you add some new goodies to your emotional toolbox.

Worried about the cost? It's possible to afford therapy on any budget.

19. Find a self-care ritual
It's easy to neglect self-care in a fast-paced world. But trying to find time to nurture yourself as much as you can is important in supporting your body's responsibilities of carrying your thoughts, passions, and spirit through this world.

Maybe it's unwinding your workweek with a long, hot bath. Or it may be adopting a skincare routine that makes you feel indulgent. Or it could be simply setting aside a night to put on your softest jammies and watch a movie from start to finish.

Whatever it is, make time for it. Put it in your planner if you must, but try to make it a priority to do it.

Monthly habits
You might want to give these monthly habits to improve your happiness a try.

20. Give back
If you find that giving daily compliments provides a needed boost to your mood, consider making a monthly routine of giving back on a larger scale.

Maybe that's helping out at a food bank on the third weekend of every month or offering to watch your friend's kids one night per month.

21. Take yourself out
No one to go out with? Well, what rule says you can't go out alone?

Consider going to your favorite restaurant, taking in a movie, or going on that trip you've always dreamed of.

Even if you're a social butterfly, spending some deliberate time alone can help you reconnect with the activities that truly make you happy.

22. Create a thought list
You arrive for an appointment with 10 minutes to spare. What do you do with that time? Pick up your cell phone to scroll through social media. Worry about the busy week you have ahead of you?

Trying to take control of your thoughts during these brief windows of time can offer benefits.

At the start of each month, make a short list of happy memories or things you're looking forward to on a small piece of paper or your phone.

When you find yourself waiting for a ride, standing in line at the grocery store, or just with a few minutes to kill, break out the list. You can even use it when you're just generally feeling down and need to change up your thoughts.

Yearly habits
Try following habits once a year or more to reflect and plan for happiness.

23. Take time to reflect
While the start of a new year is a good time to stop and take inventory of your life, you can set up yearly habits at any point in the year. Try setting aside some time to catch up with yourself the way you would with an old friend:

How are you doing?
What have you been up to?
Are you happier than you were a year ago?

But try to avoid judging yourself too harshly for your answers. You've made it to another year, and that's a reason to celebrate.

If you find that your mood hasn't improved much over the last year, consider talking with a doctor or mental health professional. You might be dealing with depression or even an underlying physical condition that's affecting your mood.

24. Reevaluate your goals
People change, so try thinking about where you're heading and consider if that's still where you want to go. There's no shame in changing your plans.

Let go of any goals that no longer serve you, even if they sound nice on paper.

25. Take care of your body
You've likely heard this before, including several times in this article. Your physical and mental health are closely intertwined.

As you build habits to improve your happiness, it's important to follow up with routine appointments to help take care of your body, such as:

seeing a primary care physician for an annual physical
discussing and addressing any chronic health conditions with a healthcare professional and seeing recommended specialists if needed
seeing a dentist for an oral cleaning and dental exam, and follow up as recommended
by getting your vision checked
26. Let go of grudges
This can often be easier said than done. But remembering that you are not necessarily doing it for another person or other people may help you be more open to beginning the process.

Sometimes, offering forgiveness or dropping a grudge is more about self-care than compassion for others.

Take stock of your relationships with others. Are you harboring any resentment or ill will toward someone? If so, consider reaching out to them to bury the hatchet.

This does not have to be a reconciliation. You may just need to end the relationship and move on.

If reaching out is not an option, try getting your feelings out in a letter. You don't even have to send it to them. Just getting your feelings out of your mind and into the world can be freeing. You can even shred the letter afterward if you want to.

27. Plan a trip

With an ever-hectic schedule, sometimes it's easy to forget to schedule something else that's crucial to your well-being: time off.

You can reap even more benefits by planning a trip, whether it's close to home or somewhere further away.

What's more, research also backs both the mental and physical benefits of taking that much-needed vacation. In one such study, researchers looked at stress and heart rate as it relates to taking a vacation. They found that not only did the vacation itself reduce stress, but the weeks leading up to that planned trip had similar effects.